A Special Gift

For:

_____

From:

_____

Date:

_____

My Sister, My Friend

Brownlow

Brownlow Publishing Company, Inc.

Little Treasures
Miniature Books

Angels of Friendship

Baby's First Little Bible

Dear Teacher

Faith

For My Secret Pal

From Friend to Friend

Golden Moments

No Friend Like a Sister

For there is no friend like a sister,
In calm or stormy weather,
To cheer one on the tedious way,
To fetch one if one goes astray,
To lift one if one totters down,
To strengthen whilst one stands.

Christina Rossetti

One of life's major mistakes is
being the last member in the
family to get the flu—after all
the sympathy has run out.

Without hearts
there is no home.

Lord Byron

No life is so strong and complete,
But it yearns for the smile
of a friend.

Wallace Bruce

There can be no situation in life in which the conversation of my dear sister will not administer some comfort to me.

Lady Mary Wortley Montagu

My best friend is the one who brings out the best in me.

Henry Ford

Often, in old age, they become each other's chosen and most happy companions. In addition to their shared memories of childhood and of their relationship to each other's children, they share memories of the same home, the same homemaking style, and the same small prejudices about housekeeping that carry the echoes of their mother's voice.

Margaret Mead

Family faces are magic mirrors.
Looking at people who belong
to us, we see the past,
present and future.

Gail Lumet Buckley

A true sister is a friend who
listens with her heart.

Anonymous

When
friends meet,
hearts warm.

Proverb

My sister! my sweet sister!
if a name
Dearer and purer were,
it should be thine.

Lord Byron

Salem, Jany, 15, 1767

Dear Sister,
Your kind letter
I receiv'd today
and am greatly rejoiced
to [hear] you
are all so well.
I was very uneasy
at not hearing from you,
indeed my dear Sister
the Winter never seem'd
so tedious to me in the World.

I daily count the days
between this and the time
I may probably see you.
I could never feel
so comfortable as
I at present do,
if I thought I should
spend another Winter here.
Indeed my Sister
I cannot bear the thought
of staying here
so far from
all my Friends if

Mr. Cranch can
do as well nigher.
I would give a great deal
only to know I was
within Ten Miles of you
if I could not see you.
Our children will never
seem so natural to each other
as if they liv'd where
they could see
one another oftener....

*Letter from Mary Smith Cranch
to her sister, Abigail Adams*

If a friend is in trouble, don't annoy him by asking if there is anything you can do. Think up something appropriate and do it.

Edgar Watson Howe

Men live by forgetting—women live on memories.

T. S. Eliot

Heirlooms we don't have in our family. But stories we've got.

Rose Chernin

As Jesus and his disciples were on their way, he came to a village where a woman named Martha opened her home to him. She had a sister called Mary, who sat at the Lord's feet listening to what he said. But Martha was distracted by all the preparations that had to be made. She came to him and asked, "Lord, don't you care that

my sister has left me to do
the work by myself?
Tell her to help me!"
"Martha, Martha,"
the Lord answered,
"you are worried and upset
about many things,
but only one thing is needed.
Mary has chosen what is better,
and it will not be
taken away from her."
Luke 10:38-42

She Touched Hearts

There was little of patronizing
benevolence about her;
her earnest kindness,
her active goodness,
darting at once to the truth
and right of things, touched
hearts. She never indulged
in verbal sentimentalism.
Her part in
the world was deeds.

Dinah Maria Mulock

Gone are those three,
those sisters rare
With wonder-lips and eyes ashine.
One was wise, and one was fair.
And one was mine.

Arthur Davison Ficke

Friendship with oneself is
all-important because without it
one cannot be friends with
anyone else in the world.

Eleanor Roosevelt

One is not born a woman,
one becomes one.

Simone de Beauvoir

We wove a web of childhood
A web of sunny air…

Charlotte Brontë

A sister is both your mirror—
and your opposite.

Elizabeth Fishel

The most I can do for my friend is simply to be his friend. I have no wealth to bestow upon him. If he knows that I am happy in loving him he will want no other reward. Is not friendship divine in this?

Lavatin

Family jokes, though rightly cursed by strangers, are the bond that keeps most families alive.

Stella Benson

Sisterhood is powerful.

Robin Morgan

Treat your friends like family and
your family like friends.

Proverb

God gave us memories that we
might have roses in December.

James M. Barrie

All Grown Up

Is the world all grown up?
Is childhood dead?
Or is there not in the bosom
of the wisest and the best
some of the child's heart left,
to respond to its
earlier enchantments.

Charles Lamb

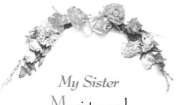

My Sister

My sister and
my sister's child,
Myself and children three,
Will fill the chaise;
so you must ride
On horseback after we.

William Cowper

If we would build on a sure foundation in friendship, we must love our friends for their sakes rather than for our own; we must look at their truth to themselves full as much as their truth to us.

Charlotte Brontë

I've got a woman's ability to stick to a job and get on with it when everyone else walks off and leaves it.

Margaret Thatcher

Friends, Brothers and Sisters

The Bible says that friends are
supposed to love all the time,
and that a brother is born
for adversity. Well, we all know
my brother has certainly
given me a lot of adversity.
But maybe that's not
what it meant.

But what about a sister?
What is a sister born for?
My sister was born to be

the rock of our family.
Even before Mother died
and Daddy got old, she was
the one we depended on.
She was the one who always
sent the special cards
on my birthday—
and every other occasion.
She loved cards and holidays
and family times.
She was the one who
made sure our little brother

didn't get left out of
the family gatherings.

She was the one who
showed me what women
of faith look like;
she put skin and flesh and life
on those old stories
of women in the Bible.
She taught me how to live.

She made me proud
of our family.

Caroline Burns

Those who love deeply
never grow old;
they may die of old age,
but they die young.
Sir Arthur Wing Pinero

True friends don't
coddle your weaknesses,
they encourage
your strengths.

One recipe for friendship is the right mixture of commonality and difference. You've got to have enough in common so that you understand each other and enough difference so that there is something to exchange.

Robert Weiss

A kindhearted woman gains respect.

Proverbs 11:16

Within our family there was
no such thing as a person
who did not matter.
Second cousins thrice
removed mattered. We knew—
and thriftily made use of—
everybody's middle name.
We knew who was buried where.
We all mattered,
and the dead most of all.

Shirley Abbott

We have been friends together
in sunshine and shade.

Caroline Norton

How vast a memory has Love!

Alexander Pope

According to popular myth, sisters exist on the same side of the closed door, sharing teddy bears and secrets in the privacy of a common bedroom.

Marianne Paul

What did the Colonel's Lady think?
Nobody ever knew.
Somebody asked the
Sergeant's Wife,
An' she told 'em true!
When you get to a man in the case,
They're like as a row of pins—
For the Colonel's Lady an'
Judy O'Grady
Are sisters under their skins!

Rudyard Kipling

We are so very rich if we know
just a few people in a way
in which we know no others.

Catherine Bramwell-Booth

The ideal of friendship
is to feel as one,
while remaining two.

Madame Swetchine

Friend

I would empty thy chalice
of heartache and pain,
Would freshen thy desert
with flowers and rain,
Would draw out the bitter
and pour in the sweet,
And remove every thorn from
the way of thy feet;

Would sing in the gladness
of summer and bloom,
And sing out the sadness
of winter and gloom,
Would lessen thy load
by enlarging thy life,
I would sing back repose,
and would sing away strife.

Charles Coke Woods

How dear
to this heart
are the scenes
of my childhood,
When fond
recollection
presents them
to view!

Samuel Woodworth

Letter of Elizabeth Barrett Browning to Her Sisters

I thank and bless you my dearest Henrietta and Arabel . . my own dearest kindest sisters!— What I suffered in reaching Orleans,—at last holding all these letters in my hands, can only be measured by my deep gratitude to you, and by

the tears and kisses I
spent upon every line of
what you wrote to me . .
dearest kindest that you are.....
My thoughts cling to you all,
and will not leave their hold.
Dearest Henrietta and Arabel
let me be as ever and for ever

Your fondly attached
Ba

The
greatest gift
we can give
one another
is rapt
attention
to one
another's
existence.

Sue Atchley Ebaugh

My Friend

The desire for friendship is
strong in every human heart.
We crave the companionship
of those who understand.
The nostalgia of life presses,
we sigh for "home," and
long for the presence of
one who sympathizes
with our aspirations,
comprehends our hopes,
and is able to partake of our joys.

Anonymous

A thought
is not our own
until we impart it
to another,
and the confessional
seems to be
a crying need
of every human soul.

She wore age so gracefully,
so carelessly, that there was a
sacred beauty about her faded
cheek more lovely and lovable
than all the bloom of her youth.
Happy woman who was not
afraid of growing old.

Dinah Maria Mulock

Let friend trust friend,
and love demand love's like.

Robert Browning

She had come to be a friend and companion such as few possessed—intelligent, well-informed, useful, gentle, knowing all the ways of the family, interested in all its concerns, and peculiarly interested in Emma, in every pleasure, every scheme of hers; one to whom Emma could speak every thought as it arose, and who had such an affection for her as could never find fault.

Jane Austen

Friendship is love
with understanding.

Ancient Proverb

We must strengthen, defend,
preserve and comfort each other.
We must love one another.

John Winthrop

Whether women are better than
men I cannot say—but I can say
they are certainly no worse.

Golda Meir

One Heart, One Mind

Make us of one heart and mind,
Courteous, merciful, and kind;
Lowly, meek in thought and word,
Ne'er by fretful passion stirred.

Free from anger, free from pride,
Let us thus in God abide;
All the depth of love express,
All the height of holiness.

Charles Wesley

Sisterly love is,
of all sentiments,
the most abstract.

Ugo Betti

One can bear grief, but
it takes two to be glad.

Elbert Hubbard

Then speak no ill, but lenient be
To others' failings as your own.
If you're the first a fault to see,
Be not the first to
make it known;
For life is but a passing day;
No lips can tell how
brief the stay.
Be earnest in the
search of good,
And speak of all
the best we may.

What families
have in common
the world around
is that they
are the place
where people learn
who they are
and how to
be that way.

Jean Illsley Clarke

The family—that dear octopus
from whose tentacles we never
quite escape, nor, in our inmost
hearts, ever quite wish to.

Dodie Smith

I hold this task to be the
highest task for a bond between
two people; that each protects
the solitude of the other.

Rainer Maria Rilke

My Sister

My sister!
With that thrilling word
Let thoughts
unnumbered wildly spring!
What echoes in
my heart are stirred,
While thus I touch
the trembling string.

Margaret Davidson

Your beauty...should be that
of your inner self, the unfading
beauty of a gentle and quiet spirit,
which is of great worth
in God's sight.

1 Peter 3:3-4

It's a great comfort
to have an artistic sister.

Louisa May Alcott

A perfect sister I am not,
But I'm thankful for
the one I've got.

Anonymous

There is no time
like the old time,
when you and I
were young!

Oliver Wendell Holmes

My sister Emily loved the moors. Flowers brighter than the rose bloomed in the blackest of the heath for her; out of a sullen hollow in a livid hill-side, her mind could make an Eden. She found in the bleak solitude many and dear delights; and not the least and best-loved was—liberty. Liberty was the breath of Emily's nostrils.

Charlotte Brontë

I have learned that
to have a good friend is
the purest of all God's gifts,
for it is a love that has
no exchange of payment.

Farmer

A sister is a gift of God,
sent from above to make life
worthwhile here below.

Anonymous

You're my friend—
What a thing friendship is,
world without end!
How it gives the heart
and soul a stir-up!

Robert Browning

Where we love is home,
Home that our feet may leave,
but not our hearts.

Oliver Wendell Holmes

Call it a clan, call it a network,
call it a tribe, call it a family.
Whatever you call it,
whoever you are,
you need one.

Jane Howard

In thee my soul
shall own combined
The sister and the friend.

Catherine Killigrew

When Doren was three years old she informed our parents she had to have a baby sister. A year later I was born. Doren often reminded me I had her to thank for this. Was I supposed to feel grateful, needed, loved? I never quite knew, but I know I believed it was my sister's idea that I come into being. I came into the world, then, Doren's child.

Cathy Arden

*And God
Created Sisters*

It wasn't on the
first day of creation,
or on any of
those first six days,
but God did
create sisters
and they are
thereby special.

Loyal friendship
Pure and true,
Such is what
I feel for you.

Two are better than one,
because they have a good return
for their work: If one falls down,
his friend can help him up.

Ecclesiastes 4:9-10

Oh better than the minting
Of a gold-crowned king
Is the safe-kept memory
Of a lovely thing.

Sara Teasdale

The Seven Ages of Women

The seven ages
of women are:
The first age is a baby,
then an infant,
then a miss,
then she's
a young woman,
a young woman,
a young woman,
a young woman.

Sisters is probably the most competitive relationship within the family, but once the sisters are grown, it becomes the strongest relationship.

Margaret Mead

The true test of friendship is to be able to sit or walk with a friend for an hour in perfect silence without wearying of one another's company.

Dinah Maria Mulock

A true friend
is forever a friend.
Proverb

Bringing up a family
should be an adventure,
not an anxious discipline
in which everybody is
constantly graded
for performance.
Milton R. Sapirstein

A woman should always
stand by a woman.

Euripides

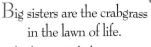

Big sisters are the crabgrass
in the lawn of life.

Charles M. Schulz, Peanuts

Sisters and friends
are God's life preservers.

Anonymous

Sisters in Harmony

Celestine and Hortense
had been drawn closely together
in affection since they had
come to live under the
same roof, and they formed
virtually one household....
The two sisters-in-law stayed
at home and looked after
their children together, and
this had created a bond

between them. They had come
to be so close to each other that
they spoke their thoughts aloud.
They presented a touching
picture of two sisters in harmony,
one happy, the other sad. The
unhappy sister, beautiful,
charged with overflowing vitality,
lively, gay, and quick witted,
in appearance belied her
actual situation; while the sober

Celestine, so gentle and calm,
as equable as reason itself,
habitually reflective and
thoughtful, would have made
an observer believe that she
had some secret sorrow.
Perhaps the contrast between
them contributed to their warm
friendship: each found in the
other what she lacked in herself.

Honoré de Balzac

Sweet is the smile of home;
the mutual look
When hearts are of each
other sure.

John Keble

If you want an accounting of your
worth, count your friends.

Merry Browne

A ministering angel
shall my sister be.

Shakespeare

Dear Sister

Yet still my fate permits
me this relief,
To write to lovely Delia
all my grief.
To you alone I venture
to complain;
From others hourly strive
to hide my pain.

*Abigail Colman Dennie
to her sister*

There is no folly equal to that
of throwing away friendship,
in a world where
friendship is so rare.

Bulwer-Lyton

Still are the thoughts
to memory dear.

Sir Walter Scott

Heavenly Fire

There is in every true woman's
heart a spark of heavenly fire,
which lies dormant in the broad
daylight of prosperity, but which
kindles up and beams and blazes
in the dark hour of adversity.

Washington Irving

The desire to be and have a sister is a primitive and profound one that may have everything or nothing to do with the family a woman is born to. It is a desire to know and be known by someone who shares blood and body, history and dreams, common ground and the unknown adventures of the future, darkest secrets and the glassiest beads of truth.

Elizabeth Fishel

Home was quite a place
when people stayed there.

E. B. White

There's a special kind of
freedom sisters enjoy. Freedom
to share innermost thoughts,
to ask a favor, to show their
true feelings. The freedom
to simply be themselves.

Anonymous

Woman to Woman

Likewise, teach the older women
to be reverent in the way they live,
not to be slanderers or addicted to
much wine, but to teach what
is good. Then they can train the
younger women to love their
husbands and children, to be self-
controlled and pure, to be busy at
home, to be kind, and to be subject
to their husbands, so that no one
will malign the word of God.

Titus 2:3-5

To My Sister

My sister! ('tis a wish of mine)
Now that our morning meal
is done,
Make haste, your morning
task resign;
Come forth and feel the sun.

One moment now
may give us more
Than years of toiling reason;
Our minds shall drink

at every pore
The spirit of the season.

Then come, my Sister!
Come, I pray,
With speed put on
your woodland dress;
And bring no book:
for this one day
We'll give to idleness.

William Wordsworth
To My Sister

True friends don't spend time
gazing into each other's eyes.
They may show great tenderness
toward each other, but they
face in the same direction—
toward common projects,
interests, goals—above all,
toward a common Lord.

C. S. Lewis

It is only the women whose eyes
have been washed clear with tears
who get the broad vision that
makes them little sisters
to all the world.

Dorothy Dix

A family is a unit composed
not only of children, but of men,
women, an occasional animal,
and the common cold.

Ogden Nash

Being with people you like and respect is so meaningful. Perhaps you have known some of them most of your life. Having friends around for a pleasant evening is one of life's most cherished joys as far as I am concerned. But when those with me are fellow believers how much greater that joy is, for we know that it will be rekindled, one day, in eternity.

James Stewart

Art Credits

Cover: Mary Evans Picture Library/
Jeffrey Morgan

Endpapers: Mary Evans Picture Library/
Sueddeutsche Zeitung Photo

This book has been bound using handcraft methods and Smyth-sewn to ensure durability.

Designed by Susan Van Horn.

Written by Joelle Herr.

Edited by Jennifer Leczkowski.

The text was set in Adobe Garamond, and Belwe.